W. YOU
Rather
Challenge
Game

Volume 2

Would You Rather Challenge Game Rules

1. One player is asked a question at one time.
2. Once he or she has answered the question, the rest of the players answer the same question.
3. If the majority is in agreement with the player, then he or she gets a point.
4. The poll about the answer to the question should be anonymous to ensure fair play.
5. The person with the most points wins!

Would you rather sneeze
100 times a day or go to
the bathroom in your pants
in public once a year?

Would you rather have a
snowball fight or a water
balloon fight?

Would you rather always be tired or always be grumpy?

Would you rather have pickles or apples or on your pizza?

Would you rather eat a live bug or a dead worm?

Would you rather have cake every day of the year except your birthday, or only have cake on your birthday?

Would you rather stay up really late or wake up really early?

Would you rather live with your whole family in a tiny house for a year or in a submarine for two months?

Would you rather always be too busy or always feel bored?

Would you rather have a pet panda bear or a pet zebra?

Would you rather live a long life in poverty or a short life with wealth?

Would you rather have a tree growing out of the floor in your living room or have no trees in your yard?

Would you rather have all of your emails for the next two months made public or have your text messages read by everyone?

Would you rather fly a kite or swing on a swing?

Would you rather have your own boat or your own plane?

Would you rather teach kindergarten or a college class?

Would you rather have a giant billboard in your front yard or a giant windmill?

Would you rather have your hardboiled eggs be slightly runny in the center or always have green yolks?

Would you rather donate your money or time during the holidays?

Would you rather have syrup or have fruit with whipped cream on your pancakes?

Would you rather have the ability to read other people's minds or the ability to see into the future?

Would you rather have an pool in your backyard or in a special room of your house?

Would you rather always have your house's windows open a little bit or never open at all?

Would you rather live in a very nice barn or a small house?

Would you rather serve lunch in the hospital or school cafeteria?

Would you rather always have a bitter taste in your mouth or always smell a skunk?

Would you rather get every new Lego set or every new video game system?

Would you rather drink warm carrot juice or eat cold tomato soup?

Would you rather have a million dollars in pennies or a million dollars worth of candy?

Would you rather have snow every day during holiday break or not have any snow at all?

Would you rather be a secret service agent for the president or be a superhero that never gets recognition?

Would you rather be a tow truck driver or a monster truck driver?

Would you rather parachute into the Grand Canyon or high dive into a deep swimming pool?

Would you rather never have to take a shower but still always smell nice or never have to go to the doctor but still be healthy?

Would you rather have the only meat you eat be fried chicken or hamburger?

Would you rather eat candy corn every day or candy canes every day?

Would you rather wear a swimsuit in a snowstorm or a snowsuit on a very hot day?

?

Would you rather have a magic button that made your parents stop talking or a magic button that made your siblings stop being mean?

Would you rather live where it is always dark outside or always light outside?

Would you rather have a picnic in a park or on the beach?

Would you rather get everywhere on a skate board or on a bicycle?

Would you rather have a robot who does all your chores or a self-driving car?

Would you rather have a magic carpet or a see-through submarine?

Would you rather go to a movie or have a backyard fire with s'mores?

Would you rather have a house next to your parent's house or live with your parents in a house that's twice as big as the one you live in now?

Would you rather have to eat only cold foods all winter long or eat only hot foods all summer long?

Would you rather have a water balloon fight or a pillow fight?

Would you rather experience an awesome waterslide or an awesome zip line?

Would you rather drink milk or tea with every meal?

Would you rather be able to sing like a diva or play the guitar in a famous country band?

Would you rather ride a
motorcycle in the rain or
ride in an open convertible
in a blizzard?

Would you rather your office
always smelled like gravy or
always smelled like coffee?

Would you rather eat any flavor of ice cream for one week of summer or only vanilla-flavored ice cream for an entire summer?

Would you rather be able to smell only bad-smelling things or never be able to smell again?

Would you rather volunteer to make 1,000 Christmas cookies or to decorate 100 Christmas trees?

Would you rather have a $100 every day or three extra hours in each day?

Would you rather ride your bike in the pouring rain or on slippery snow?

Would you rather always wear sweat pants or always wear blue jeans?

Would you rather have a new candy named after you or a newly discovered animal named after you?

Would you rather have no Winter Break or have no Spring Break?

Would you rather eat only holiday food or watch only holiday movies?

Would you rather be on an airplane between two arguing passengers or next to a screaming infant?

Would you rather live for a year in the hottest place or the coldest place on earth?

Would you rather visit far-away family or far-away friends?

Would you rather have a job that requires very little work but it was boring or work very hard at an interesting job?

Would you rather live in a tree house the rest of your life or live on a boat house the rest of your life?

Would you rather watch a fireworks display or a circus performance?

Would you rather eat a stick of butter or four tablespoons of salt?

Would you rather have to sew all your own clothes or grow all your own food?

Would you rather switch careers every five years entirely or stay in your career field forever?

Would you rather swim in a lake or in the ocean?

Would you rather go to the school only in the summer or go to school during the rest of the year and have summers off?

Would you rather live on a large boat in a busy harbor or in a large cabin far from any neighbors?

Would you rather have a freezer that has all your favorite ice cream flavors or one that has a different flavor every day?

Would you rather work untangling Christmas lights or work as a mall Santa?

Would you rather always have to walk in soggy grass and get wet socks, or always have a tiny pebble in your shoe?

Would you rather have super strong arms or super strong legs?

Would you rather have a video arcade or a library inside your home?

Would you rather go back in time to meet your great-great grandparents, or go in the future to meet your great-great grandchildren?

Would you rather have to pull Santa's sleigh for workouts or lift pumpkins?

Would you rather get hit in the back with a rotten tomato or have a pie thrown in your face?

Would you rather work at a desk in a cubicle or have an outdoor job?

Would you rather get to name a newly discovered tree or a newly discovered fish?

Would you rather have a jetpack or a jet?

Would you rather have as many chips or as much candy as you want?

Would you rather have butterfly wings or a horse tail?

Would you rather always
wear socks to your knees
or never wear socks again?

Would you rather be kept up
at night by loud music or by
a baby crying?

Would you rather be able to talk to birds or talk to squirrels?

Would you rather eat bananas that were always too ripe or not ripe enough?

Would you rather have an amazing tree house or your whole backyard be a trampoline?

Would you rather have a noisy neighbor or a nosy neighbor?

Would you rather be on a game show or star in a soap opera?

Would you rather be a great painter or an amazing dancer?

Would you rather be a stand-up comedian or a concert pianist?

Would you rather eat an entire cake or an entire carton of ice cream?

Would you rather play the tuba or play the accordion?

Would you rather have your first child when you are 21-years old or when you are 41-years old?

Would you rather have a giant backyard with no trees or a small yard with a big climbing tree?

Would you rather always have to wear jeans in hot weather or always have to wear shorts in cold weather?

Would you rather have no sense of smell or smell everything around you with extra ability?

Would you rather be a maid for the dirtiest person in the world or be a chef for someone who eats all day?

Would you rather have chocolate chips or brown sugar in your oatmeal?

Would you rather have green hair or orange eyes?

Would you rather have a soda machine or a snack machine in your kitchen?

Would you rather have Thanksgiving at the White House or with your family?

Would you rather have a new shirt appear in your closet every morning or a new pair of shoes appear in your closet once a week?

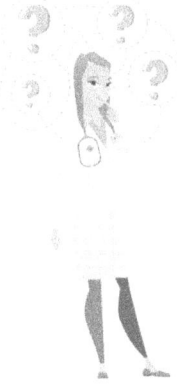

Would you rather move to a different city or move to a different country?

Would you rather exercise regularly or eat a healthy diet?

Would you rather wake up with a dog tail or deer antlers?

Would you rather wear cowboy boots or flip-flops year round?

Would you rather stay up all night helping a family member with a problem or babysit a baby that will not stop crying?

Would you rather always have to say everything that you are thinking or never speak again?

Would you rather have pancakes every day for breakfast or pizza every day for dinner?

Would you rather have your grandmother's hairstyle or her first name?

Would you rather mow the grass or rake the leaves?

Would you rather have all of your emails for the next two months made public or have your text messages read by everyone?

Would you rather be in a hot dog eating contest or in a donut eating contest?

Would you rather have no cell phone or no computer?

Would you rather wake up with an elephant trunk or a giraffe neck?

Would you rather be a police officer or a fire fighter?

Would you rather have a hamburger or a taco for breakfast?

Would you rather have to crawl everywhere or run everywhere?

Would you rather be able to shrink down to the size of an ant any time you wanted to or be able to grow to the size of a giraffe anytime you wanted to?

Would you rather wear no shoes for an entire year or watch no TV for an entire year?

Would you rather have a room with whiteboard walls or a room where the ceiling is like a planetarium?

Would you rather have only two close friends or many acquaintances?

Would you rather take the elevator or the escalator?

Would you rather have no internet or no air-conditioning and heating?

Would you rather live on the moon or live on Mars?

Would you rather go on vacation to a new country every summer or get an extra three weeks of summer break?

Would you rather win 10,000 dollars in the lottery or never have to buy food again?

Would you rather be a chef
or a waiter?

Would you rather be able to
swim as well as a dolphin or
fly as well as an eagle?

Would you rather go on the vacation of a lifetime or get the best computer ever?

Would you rather have sand in your shoes or sand in your hair?

Would you rather have a twenty dollar bill or twenty dollars in coins?

Would you rather wear the same clean outfit every day, or always have a noticeable stain on whatever you wore?

Would you rather live in a cabin in Alaska or a straw hut on a tropical island?

Would you rather have ten cavities or get ten shots in the arm?

Would you rather mow the lawn or shovel snow?

Would you rather camp in a tent or a in a pop-up camper?

Would you rather only be allowed to wear long-sleeved sweaters or sleeveless shirts?

Would you rather own a pirate ship and crew or a private jet with a pilot and infinite fuel?

Would you rather play the trumpet or the saxaphone?

Would you rather live in the desert or on a deserted island?

Would you rather that all fruit tasted like watermelon or like pineapple?

Would you rather own a movie theater or a bed & breakfast?

Would you rather be friends with someone who has lots of money or someone with a good heart?

Would you rather be given $3 every day for the rest of your life or be given $1,000 only once?

Would you rather wear
mismatched clothes that fit
comfortably, or wear a nice
looking outfit that feels
uncomfortable?

Would you rather be a
detective or a firefighter?

Would you rather sleep in a tent or in a camper?

Would you rather be a turkey farmer or a pumpkin farmer?

Would you rather stay up
all night watching cartoons
or skip a day of school?

Would you rather visit every
country in the world or be
able to play any musical
instrument?

Would you rather be the smartest kid in school and get good grades or be the most popular kid in school and get bad grades?

Would you rather swim in a pool of Jello-o or swim in a pool of pudding?

Would you rather eat a hot dog in a hamburger bun or eat a hamburger in a hot dog bun?

Would you rather be unable to talk ever again or only be able to speak at a loud volume whenever you speak?

Would you rather be wildly popular on social media or be the host of an extremely popular podcast?

Would you rather always take cold showers or never get enough sleep?

Would you rather set the table before dinner or clean up after dinner?

Would you rather be able to read and remember any book in two minutes or be able to cook any meal in two minutes?

Would you rather never have to read another book for school or never have to study for another test?

Would you rather deliver the newspaper at 5 AM every day or at 5 PM every day?

Would you rather go to your class reunion and nobody remember who you are or have everybody comment on how old you look?

Would you rather go to the movies or go to a waterpark?

Would you rather always wait in long lines or always have to shop for groceries in the middle of the night?

Would you rather always have your food be a little too salty or use no seasoning at all?

Would you rather win one million dollars today or ten million dollars in ten years?

Would you rather spend two months living in a hospital or two months living in a tent?

Would you rather wear a coat to bed every night or sleep with shoes and socks on every night?

Would you rather work construction on a high rise building or install pipes in the sewer?

Would you rather eat a bagel or an English muffin?

Would you rather always be woken up by a rooster or by a police siren?

Would you rather have to mix up all your food before you eat it or eat everything with a spoon?

Would you rather eat a raw onion or eat a big bowl of boiled spinach?

Would you rather live on the first floor or the 20th floor with no elevator?

Would you rather be a professional golfer or bowler?

Would you rather work alone on a school project or work with others on a school project?

Would you rather have the power to run as fast as the speed of light, or the power to walk through walls?

Would you rather wake up
with wings instead of arms
or a trunk instead of a
nose?

Would you rather go
through a car wash with the
windows half-way down or
take an ice- cold shower?

Would you rather everything in your house be one color or every single wall and door be a different color?

?

Would you rather sail around the world or fly to the moon?

Would you rather be able to rewind time or freeze time?

Would you rather only be able to wear your swimsuit for the rest of your life or only be able to wear pants and a winter coat?

Would you rather meet a superhero or a cartoon character?

Would you rather eat your favorite food every day or find two dollars under your pillow every morning?

Would you rather surf in shark-infested waters or jump free fall with a parachute into the Grand Canyon?

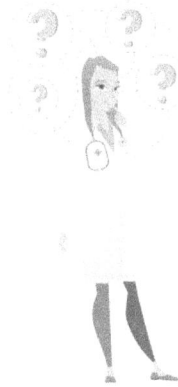

Would you rather be rich and alone or be poor and find true love?

Would you rather ride in a rusted car that never breaks down or a sports car that breaks down once a month?

?

Would you rather eat cheese pizza or a supreme pizza?

Would you rather be able to breathe underwater or be able to run on top of water?

Would you rather play chess or Sorry?

Would you rather live 100 years ago or 100 years in the future?

Would you rather have eyes that change color with your mood or hair that changes color with the temperature?

Would you rather always have to enter rooms backwards or always have to somersault out?

Would you rather always walk on the ceiling or always crawl on the floor?

Thanks For Playing!

CPSIA information can be obtained
at www.ICGtesting.com
Printed in the USA
BVHW042146101121
621338BV00012B/477

9 781694 938688